BY KATHRYN WALTON

VISIT
AMERICA'S
NATIONAL
PARKS!

VISIT

ACADIA
NATIONAL PARK!

Enslow
PUBLISHING

Please visit our website, www.enslow.com. For a free color catalog of all our high-quality books, call toll free 1-800-398-2504 or fax 1-877-980-4454.

Library of Congress Cataloging-in-Publication Data
Names: Walton, Kathryn, 1993- author.
Title: Visit Acadia National Park! / Kathryn Walton.
Description: Buffalo, NY : Enslow Publishing, [2025] | Series: Visit America's national parks! | Includes index.
Identifiers: LCCN 2024004352 (print) | LCCN 2024004353 (ebook) | ISBN 9781978540545 (library binding) | ISBN 9781978540538 (paperback) | ISBN 9781978540552 (ebook)
Subjects: LCSH: Acadia National Park (Me.)–Juvenile literature.
Classification: LCC F27.M9 W358 2025 (print) | LCC F27.M9 (ebook) | DDC 974.1/45–dc23/eng/20240129
LC record available at https://lccn.loc.gov/2024004352
LC ebook record available at https://lccn.loc.gov/2024004353

Published in 2025 by
Enslow Publishing
2544 Clinton Street
Buffalo, NY 14224

Portions of this work were originally authored by Kathleen Connors and published as *Acadia National Park*. All new material in this edition is authored by Kathryn Walton.

Copyright © 2025 Enslow Publishing

Designer: Tanya Dellaccio Keeney
Editor: Natalie Humphrey

Photo credits: Series Art (Acadia illustration) khezy licious/Shutterstock.com; cover (photo) Zack Frank/Shutterstock.com; p. 5 (top) Jon Bilous/Shutterstock.com; p. 5 (bottom) Rainer Lesniewski/Shutterstock.com; p. 7 Darryl Brooks/Shutterstock.com; p. 9 https://upload.wikimedia.org/wikipedia/en/5/5c/George_Bucknam_Dorr_on_the_Beachcroft_Path_at_Huguenot_Head.jpg; p. 11 Danita Delimont/Shutterstock.com; p. 12 lavinak/Shutterstock.com; p. 13 Alexey Stiop/Shutterstock.com; p. 15 Allan Wood Photography/Shutterstock.com; p.7 (top) Bonnie Taylor Barry/Shutterstock.com; p. 17 (bottom) Wang LiQiang/Shutterstock.com; p. 19 Susan Natoli/Shutterstock.com.

All rights reserved. No part of this book may be reproduced in any form without permission in writing from the publisher, except by a reviewer.

Some of the images in this book illustrate individuals who are models. The depictions do not imply actual situations or events.

Printed in the United States of America

CPSIA compliance information: Batch #CSENS25: For further information contact Enslow Publishing at 1-800-398-2504.

CONTENTS

VISITING ACADIA 4

THE WABANAKI NATIVE AMERICANS 6

GEORGE B. DORR 8

ROCKEFELLER'S CARRIAGE ROADS 10

SUNRISE ON CADILLAC MOUNTAIN 12

LIGHT ON THE COAST 14

ACADIA'S PLANTS AND ANIMALS 16

SWIMMING IN ACADIA 18

ACADIA'S WEATHER 20

GLOSSARY 22

FOR MORE INFORMATION 23

INDEX 24

Words in the glossary appear in **bold** type the first time they are used in the text.

VISITING ACADIA

While Acadia National Park might not be the biggest national park in the United States, it's one you won't want to miss! Nature lovers can enjoy a hike up the tall mountains or a bike ride around the park. Visitors to Acadia National Park cross a bridge from **mainland** Maine to Mount Desert Island to get to the bigger part of the park.

Acadia National Park is one of the top 10 most-visited parks in the United States. Around 3.8 million people visited the park in 2023!

THE WABANAKI NATIVE AMERICANS

Native Americans have lived on the land that makes up Acadia National Park for over 5,000 years. Many of the Wabanaki Native Americans made their homes on Mount Desert Island where Acadia National Park is today.

Europeans first came to Mount Desert Island during the 1500s. By the 1800s, it was a common place for white people to visit. While many of the Wabanaki people now live on **reservations** elsewhere, the island is still an important place to them.

To learn more about the Wabanaki people, visitors to Acadia National Park can stop by Abbe **Museum**.

MORE TO KNOW

There are five Native American groups that now make up the Wabanaki people. These groups are the Abenaki, Maliseet, Mi'kmaq, Passamaquoddy, and Penobscot.

GEORGE B. DORR

During the 1880s, many rich European vacationers were interested in **preserving** the natural beauty of Mount Desert Island. George B. Dorr was one of these people. In 1916, Dorr gave the U.S. government the land he and others had **acquired** for preservation. Mount Desert Island became a national **monument**!

Dorr continued to acquire land and worked to make all of it into a national park. In 1919, Lafayette National Park became the first national park created east of the Mississippi River.

George B. Dorr was the first **superintendent** of Acadia National Park.

MORE TO KNOW

Lafayette National Park was renamed Acadia National Park in 1929. "Acadia" was what French explorers called parts of Maine and parts of Canada's present-day New Brunswick, Novia Scotia, Prince Edward Island, and Quebec.

ROCKEFELLER'S CARRIAGE ROADS

Between 1913 and 1940, American **philanthropist** John D. Rockefeller Jr. paid for the construction of broken-stone carriage roads in Acadia National Park. These roads were built to **withstand** the weather in Maine.

Today, more than 45 miles (72 km) of carriage roads wind through Acadia National Park. Visitors can walk, bike, snowshoe, or cross-country ski on these roads. The roads are a great way to see lots of the park, especially since many of them show off the most beautiful parts!

In total, the carriage roads cost Rockefeller $3.5 million!

MORE TO KNOW

John D. Rockefeller Jr. was very wealthy. The carriage roads were made on land he donated, or gave, and were meant only for people to walk or ride horses on.

SUNRISE ON CADILLAC MOUNTAIN

At Acadia National Park, it pays to get up early! In the fall and winter, Cadillac Mountain is the first place on the East Coast that the sun touches as it rises. If you're not an early bird, the mountain's beauty is worth seeing anyway!

If you visit Cadillac Mountain, it's important to respect the mountain and "leave no trace." This means cleaning up after yourself, being careful not to step on any plants, and leaving wild animals alone!

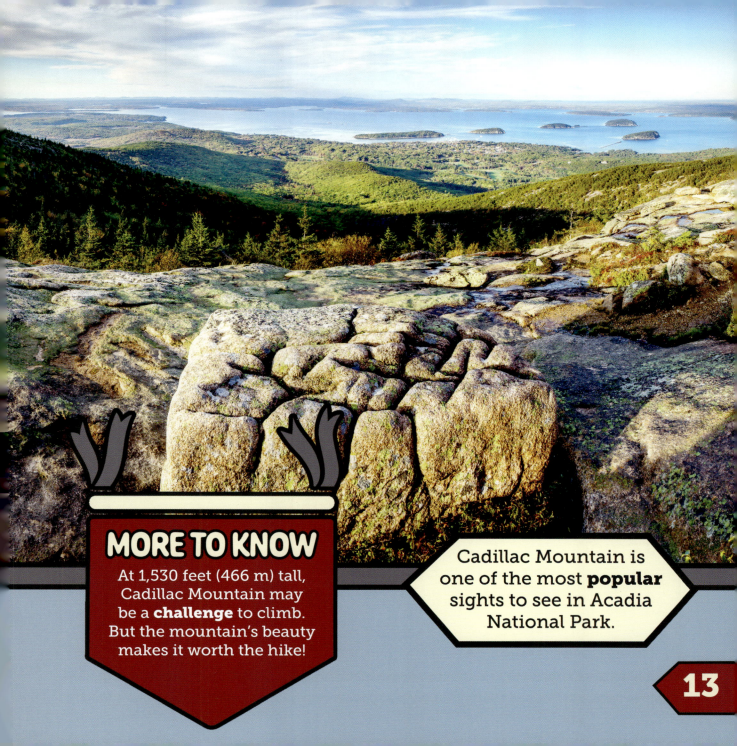

MORE TO KNOW
At 1,530 feet (466 m) tall, Cadillac Mountain may be a **challenge** to climb. But the mountain's beauty makes it worth the hike!

Cadillac Mountain is one of the most **popular** sights to see in Acadia National Park.

LIGHT ON THE COAST

The water around Acadia National Park can be deadly. The rocky coast and storms have caused many shipwrecks. To help stop this, lighthouses were built. Today, Acadia National Park operates three of these lighthouses. They still light the way for passing ships.

The most visted lighthouse in Acadia National Park is the Bass Harbor Head Lighthouse. Around 180,000 people visit Bass Harbor Head Lighthouse each year! It was built in 1858 and is the only lighthouse found on Mount Desert Island.

The Bass Harbor Head Lighthouse light shows passing ships the opening leading to Blue Hill Bay and Bass Harbor.

MORE TO KNOW

Bass Harbor Head Lighthouse was run by the U.S. Coast Guard until July 2020. Today, the lighthouse is run by the National Park Service.

ACADIA'S PLANTS AND ANIMALS

Acadia National Park protects more than 1,000 kinds of plants. Ferns, such as rock polypody, grow in cool, shady spots. About 80 kinds of freshwater plants can be found in the lakes and streams of the park. Some kinds of **marine** plants can also be found in Acadia National Park. Starflowers, lilies of the valley, and other wildflowers dot the forests too.

Acadia National Park is known for its birds! Eagles, great blue herons, and ospreys are often spotted—among many others!

FERNS

MORE TO KNOW

Some plants and animals found in Acadia are endangered, or at risk of dying out. Animals such as peregrine falcons and northern long-eared bats are listed by the United States as endangered.

Harlequin ducks, like the ones below, are a protected species in Maine. They are found in Acadia National Park.

SWIMMING IN ACADIA

If you don't want to bike, hike, or walk the trails in Acadia National Park, you can take a bus or trolley tour. You can learn a lot about the wildlife and history of the park as well as find where some of the best views are.

Even though most of the park is forested, there's also the opportunity to go whale watching, sailing on a sunset cruise, or kayaking. If you enjoy swimming, there are three great places to swim in Acadia!

Some swimming spots in Acadia may not have a **lifeguard**, so make sure to swim with an adult!

MORE TO KNOW

Sand Beach, Acadia's only saltwater and sand beach, is a popular swimming spot. If you don't want to swim in salt water, Lake Wood and Echo Lake Beach are the two freshwater beaches.

ACADIA'S WEATHER

Days in Acadia National Park during the spring and fall are commonly between 30° and 70°F (-1° and 21°C). Summer days may be as cool as 45°F (7°C) or as hot as 90°F (32°C)!

During the winter, the park is cold. If you decide to see Acadia during the winter, make sure to pack a warm coat and boots. There may be a lot of snow. Acadia National Park is the perfect place to visit all year long!

MORE TO KNOW

Around 60 inches (152.4 cm) of snow falls in Acadia National Park each year.

ACADIA NATIONAL PARK
THE FACTS

ESTABLISHED
1916 as Sieur de Monts National Monument;
later became Lafayette National Park;
renamed in 1929 as Acadia National Park

SIZE
65 square miles (168 sq km)

NUMBER OF VISITORS EACH YEAR
over 3 million each year

NATIVE WILDLIFE
eagles, owls, loons, peregrine falcons, foxes, bats, beavers, and more

NATIVE PLANTS
ferns, wildflowers, evergreen trees,
freshwater and marine plants, and more

MUST-SEE STOPS
Bass Harbor Head Lighthouse, Sieur de Monts Spring,
Cadillac Mountain, carriage roads

GLOSSARY

acquire: To get as one's own.

challenge: A test of abilities.

lifeguard: A person who watches bodies of water to make sure swimmers don't get hurt.

mainland: A landmass or the main part of a landmass.

marine: Having to do with the sea.

monument: Something built to help people remember an important event or person.

museum: A building in which things of interest are displayed.

popular: Liked by many people.

philanthropist: One who gives money for the good of others.

preserve: To keep something in its original state.

reservation: Land set aside by the U.S. government for Native Americans.

superintendent: A person in charge of managing, directing, and taking care of a place or organization.

withstand: To endure harsh or rough conditions.

FOR YOUR INFORMATION

Books

Leaf, Christina. *Acadia National Park*. Minneapolis, MN: Bellwether Media, Inc., 2023.

Nelson, Penelope. *Acadia National Park*. Minneapolis, MN: Jump!, 2020.

Websites

National Geographic Kids: Acadia National Park
www.kids.nationalgeographic.com/nature/article/acadia
Learn more about the history of Acadia National Park.

National Park Service: For Kids
www.nps.gov/acad/planyourvisit/for-kids.htm
Find out things that you can do on your visit to Acadia National Park.

Publisher's note to educators and parents: Our editors have carefully reviewed these websites to ensure that they are suitable for students. Many websites change frequently, however, and we cannot guarantee that a site's future contents will continue to meet our high standards of quality and educational value. Be advised that students should be closely supervised whenever they access the internet.

INDEX

Abbe Museum, 7

Bass Harbor Head Lighthouse, 14, 15, 21

beaches, 19

bike, 4, 10, 18

birds, 16, 21

Cadillac Mountain, 12, 13, 21

carriage roads, 10, 11, 21

Dorr, George B., 8, 9

endangered, 16, 17

hike, 4, 13, 18

Lafayette National Park, 8, 9, 21

"leave no trace," 12

lighthouses, 14

Maine, 4, 5, 9, 10, 17

Mount Desert Island, 4, 5, 6, 8, 14

name, 9, 21

plants, 16, 17, 21

Rockefeller, John D. Jr., 10, 11

Wabanaki, 6, 7

weather, 10, 20